TO: ____________________

FROM:

____

Acronyms In Action by Fee

42 power packed devotionals that will inspire you to live life on purpose for Christ!

DEDICATION:

This book is dedicated to my beautiful mother, a mighty woman of God, Mary E. Williams, who has made this all possible. It was through her that I came to know Jesus Christ as my personal savior . She is also an example of what it means to truly live life on purpose for Christ.

I also dedicate this book to my sons Dante' and Brandyn (God's gifts to me) who have taken this journey with me and continued to love me unconditionally. They have been the motivating force behind everything I've done to this point. I thank God for them.

To order copies contact:

Felicia Y. Williams at
swordsofspiritaia@yahoo.com

ISBN: 978-1-4583-3559-3

Scriptures taken from: NIV, NCV, KJV, NJKV

About the Author

Felicia Y. Williams was born in Alexander City Alabama on March 3, 1970 to Jake and Mary Williams. She is the third of four children. When she was three months old her mother and father, moved to Columbus, Ohio. Her parents separated when she was eleven years old and when she was thirteen her mother relocated to Oakland, California with she and her siblings.

Her mom instilled the principles and values of God in her and her siblings at a very early age. They attended church regularly and were very active in the youth ministry. Felicia was raised in the Baptist denomination for most of her life, however, her mother encouraged she and her siblings to believe on the word of God more so than denominational boundaries and beliefs. At the age of 14 she accepted Christ as her personal savior on Easter Sunday in April of 1984. She became a member of Discipleship Baptist Church in Oakland, California and was under the teaching and guidance of the late Pastor Leslie Smith. After moving away to Alabama for 6 years, she relocated to the Sacramento area in 2006 and considers it a blessing to be under the leadership of Doctor's Phillip and Brenda Goudeaux of Calvary Christian Center. She is the mother of two sons, Brandyn, 18 and Dante', 24, who also reside in the Sacramento area.

Felicia has experienced life's difficulties as would anyone else however, coupled with being a single mother and desiring to have more, she battled with feelings of inadequacy and loneliness. As she matured in faith, the Word and her relationship with Christ, she began the quest to seek her God-ordained purpose in life. Over the years it would begin to be revealed right before her very eyes!

In 2008 she founded and incorporated "SIG/Standing in the Gap Inc. youth ministry. This ministry focuses on reaching out to youth who are at risk. Most of the youth she serves are in out of home placement such as foster care, group homes or residential facilities. Felicia currently works as a social worker for a Foster Care agency and she does mental health counseling for youth. In 2007 she officially began to market her fashion business, Fee's Fash'N' 4U! specializing in personal shopping and fashion consulting.

Now she is honored and thrilled to introduce you to her first book "AIA/Acronyms In Action by Fee". According to Felicia "this is only the beginning! The Lord has placed so much inside of me to share with the world to encourage, empower, motivate, and enlighten men, women, boys and girls to live life on purpose for Christ! I am excited and pray that you get on board and take this journey with me."

She has also launched SOS/Swords Of the Spirit ministry in conjunction with her new book.

Websites:

SOS/Swords Of the Spirit – www.swordsofspirit.com

SIG/Standing In the Gap Inc. – www.standngap.bravehost.com

Fee's Fash'N' 4U! – www.feesfashn4u.com

<u>What is an ACRONYM?</u> – a word formed from the initial letters or groups of letters of words in a set phrase or series of words.

WHY ACRONYMS IN ACTION?

I firmly believe and am a witness to the fact that **Words have power!** When used negatively, words can **W**ound **O**ppress **R**eproach or **D**estroy. However, **in the spiritual realm, words are used as containers of Power** and are **W**ise **O**rdained **R**eputable and **D**estined because they are inspired by the Holy Spirit. Scripture confirms that *"God is not like people. He tells no lies. He is not like humans. He doesn't change his mind. When he says something, he does it. When he makes a promise, he keeps it."*– **Numbers 23:19**. God's Word is able to: heal past hurts and failures rendering one **Whole** (nothing missing, nothing broken, fullness), **Ordain** (establish/order) your future, **Redirect** your path so that you are walking in His will and purpose, God's word has the power to bring you into your **Destiny**! Words **bring the promises of God's Word into the natural realm,** and bring blessings to you and your family. However, **faith and obedience are essential** to receiving the Promises of God.

"Faith begins where the will of God is known *(Dr. Kenneth E. Hagin).*" In order to believe what the Word of God says, **you must KNOW the Word**. **God's Word contains power within itself to cause what it says to come to pass**. When used as God intended it, the Word will begin to work in your life. However it takes ACTION on your part; your faith should move you to action! You must speak it, confess it and act on it!

Speaking the Word is called "Confession." In order for the Power of God to cause something that God has promised to be manifested in this natural realm, you must speak, or confess, His Word and agree with God! Then God will back up His promise by bringing it to pass in the natural realm! You must speak the Word!

"Confession brings possession." This means that **what you desire and confess comes from the spiritual into the physical realm**. A spiritual truth takes on physical form in this world. God is a Spirit and those that worship Him must worship Him in Spirit, and in Truth! (John 4:24) The spiritual realm is higher than the natural realm. God **created all matter, and He can change it as well!**

Each acronym used has an inspiring, power packed message of encouragement. Every word is inspired and purposed to speak life & healing thus denouncing the negative forces of wickedness from prevailing in the life of all who read and believe them. The purpose of AIA is to encourage, equip, edify and empower men, women, boys and girls towards greatness in their spiritual journey here on earth.

Powerful words such as Empower, Holy, Anointed and Destined are used in a number of the acronyms.

"AIA seeks to speak life, healing, deliverance & purpose to everyone!" As the word declares in Proverbs 18:21 –"The power of life and death are in the tongue." AIA speaks **L.I.F.E**..... **L**ove, **I**nspiration, **F**aith & **E**mpowerment!

WHAT INSPIRED AIA & SOS?

Acronyms In Action/AIA was birthed at the end of 2009 through me, Fee/Felicia Y. Williams. As the Holy Spirit impressed words on my heart while reading, listening to gospel music or a message, I began writing them down, meditating on each word, defining it and looking up scripture that related to it. Afterwards I would take each letter of the base word and assign a word to it that would either highlight its meaning or assign a positive meaning to it. I noticed that the words seemed to come ALIVE thus becoming **A**ctive **L**iving **I**nspiring **V**isible & **E**mpowering! The Holy Spirit spoke Acronyms In Action to me and that is how AIA came to be!

Since AIA represents the word spoken and alive, it was only fitting that the product line would be called SOS/Swords Of the Spirit products for "The Word" warrior. Our sword of the Spirit is **the word** of God. When Jesus was tempted by Satan in the wilderness, Jesus quoted His Father's words and spoke them with authority. Consequently, each Word was like a sword-blow to Satan's head! **God has given us the authority to use His words** because we are all ambassadors of Christ. God speaks with ultimate authority in the universe. He spoke and the universe came into being from nothing. **When we speak God's word according to his will, there is no power in the universe that can withstand it!**

FOUNDATIONAL SCRIPTURE for AIA & SOS:

- **Proverbs 18:21** –"The **power of life** and death are **in the tongue**."
- **Hebrews 4:12**- For the **word of God** are **alive** and **powerful.** It is sharper than the sharpest two-edged sword, cutting between soul and spirit, between joint and marrow. It exposes our innermost thoughts and desires.

My prayer is that the consumers of SOS products will not only seek to make a fashion statement but will also become a living testimony of Christ-likeness and live a fulfilled life walking in their God-ordained purpose and destiny!

S.O.S./A.I.A. products include: Books, t-shirts, hoodies, mugs, hats, key chains, bags, buttons, sneakers, posters, and rubber wristbands and devotional materials.

Table of Contents

a.c.t.i.o.n.

SCRIPTURE: James 2:14-17: *"What good is it, my brothers, if a man claims to have faith but has no deeds? Can such faith save him? Suppose a brother or sister is without clothes and daily food. If one of you says to him, "Go, I wish you well; keep warm and well fed," but does nothing about his physical needs, what good is it? In the same way, faith by itself, if it is not accompanied by action, is dead.*

WORD DEFINED: **Action -** An act that one consciously wills and that may be characterized by physical or mental activity.

IN ACTION: **A**ctively **C**ommitted to **I**nvesting **I**n **O**thers **N**eeds

KEY WORDS:

Actively - Marked by or involving direct participation.
Committed - Bound or obligated, as under a pledge to a particular cause, action, or attitude.
Investing - To devote morally or psychologically, as to a purpose; commit.

FOOD 4 THOUGHT:

Just as a fruit tree is expected to bear fruit, God's people should produce a crop of good deeds. God has no use for people who call themselves Christians but do nothing about it. Like many people in the Bible who were God's people in name only, we are of no value if we are Christians in name only. If others can't see our faith in the way we treat them, we may not be God's people at all.

God's message hasn't changed since the Old Testament — people will be judged for their unproductive lives. God calls us to be *active* in our obedience. People who claim they believe God but don't live for God are compared to unproductive trees that will be cut down. To be productive for God, we must obey his teachings, resist temptation, actively serve and help others, and share our faith.

TAKE ACTION!

While it is true that our good deeds can never earn salvation, true faith always results in a changed life and good deeds. Paul speaks against those who try to be saved by deeds instead of true faith; James speaks against those who confuse mere intellectual assent with true faith. After all, even demons know who Jesus is, but they don't obey him (Jam 2:19). True faith involves a commitment of your whole self to God. How productive are you for God?

Today I will take action by:

A.L.I.V.E.

SCRIPTURE: Hebrews 4:12 – "For the word of God is alive and powerful. It is sharper than the sharpest two-edged sword, cutting between soul and spirit, between joint and marrow. It exposes our innermost thoughts and desires."

WORD DEFINED: **Alive -** In a state of action; in force or operation; active.

IN ACTION: **A**ctive **L**iving **I**nspiring **V**isible & **E**mpowering

KEY WORDS:
Active - causing activity or change; capable of exerting influence.
Inspiring - to give rise to, bring about, cause
Empowering - to give power or authority to; to authorize

FOOD 4 THOUGHT:
Jesus was hungry and weak after fasting for 40 days (Matthew 4:3-4), but he chose not to use his divine power to satisfy his natural desire for food. Food, hunger, and eating are good, but the timing was wrong. Jesus was in the desert to fast, not to eat. And because Jesus had given up the unlimited, independent use of his divine power in order to experience humanity fully, he wouldn't use his power to change the stones to bread.

Jesus was able to resist all of the devil's temptations because he not only knew Scripture, but he also obeyed it. Ephesians 6:17 says that God's Word is a sword to use in spiritual combat. Knowing Bible verses is an important step in helping us resist the devil's attacks, but we must also obey the Bible. Note that Satan had memorized Scripture, but he failed to obey it. Knowing and obeying the Bible helps us follow God's desires rather than the devils.

TAKE ACTION!

Word of God is not simply a collection of words from God, a vehicle for communicating ideas; it is living, life-changing, and dynamic as it works in us. With the incisiveness of a surgeon's knife, God's Word reveals who we are and what we are not. It penetrates the core of our moral and spiritual life. It discerns what is within us, both good and evil. The demands of God's Word require decisions. We must not only listen to the Word; we must also let it shape our lives.

Today I will take action by:

B·A·T·T·L·E·

SCRIPTURE: 2 Chronicles 20:15 – He said, "Listen, all you people of Judah and Jerusalem! Listen, King Jehoshaphat! This is what the LORD says: Do not be afraid! Don't be discouraged by this mighty army, for the battle is not yours, but God's.

WORD DEFINED: **Battle -** A conflict or struggle between opposing forces.

IN ACTION: **B**oldly **A**dvancing **T**rusting **T**he **L**ord to **E**quip

KEY WORDS:
Bold - not hesitating or fearful in the face of actual or possible danger.
Advance - to move or bring forward.
Trust - to rely on the integrity, strength, and ability of (God)
Equip - to furnish or provide with whatever is needed for use or for any undertaking.

FOOD 4 THOUGHT:
As the enemy bore down on Judah, God spoke through Jahaziel: "Do not be afraid or discouraged . . . . For the battle is not yours, but God's." We may not fight an enemy army, but every day we battle temptation, pressure, and "rulers . . . of this dark world" (Ephesians 6:12) who want us to rebel against God. Remember, as believers, we have God's Spirit in us. If we ask for God's help when we face struggles, God will fight for us. And God always triumphs.

TAKE ACTION!

How do we let God fight for us? (1) By realizing the battle is not ours, but God's; (2) by recognizing human limitations and allowing God's strength to work through our fears and weaknesses; (3) by making sure we are pursuing God's interests and not just our own selfish desires; (4) by asking God for help in our daily battles.

Today I will take action by:

B.U.T.T.E.R.F.L.Y.

SCRIPTURE: 2 Corinthians 5:17 – "Therefore, if anyone is in Christ, he is a new creation; the old has gone, the new has come!"

WORD DEFINED: **Butterfly -** Any of various insects of the order Lepidoptera, characteristically having slender bodies, knobbed antennae, and four broad, usually colorful wings.

IN ACTION: **B**eautiful **U**nique **T**ransformed **T**riumphant **E**mpowered **R**enewed **F**ruitful **L**oyal & **Y**ielded

KEY WORDS:

Unique - being the only one of its kind
Transformed - to change in form, appearance, or structure
Triumphant - To be victorious or successful; win
Empowered - to give power or authority to; to authorize
Renewed – To make new or as if new again; restore
Fruitful – Conducive to productivity; causing to bear in abundance the fruit of the spirit (love, joy, peace, patience, etc.)
Loyal – faithful to one's oath, commitments, or obligations
Yielded - To give over possession of, as in deference or defeat; surrender

FOOD 4 THOUGHT:

Christians are brand-new people on the *inside.* The Holy Spirit gives them new life, and they are not the same any more. We are not reformed, rehabilitated, or reeducated—we are new creations, living in vital union with Christ (Colossians 2:6-7). We are not merely turning over a new leaf; we are beginning a new life under a new Master.

TAKE ACTION!

Only when our mind is renewed by the new attitude Christ gives us are we truly transformed. If our character is like Christ's, we can be sure our behavior will honor God. Just as the caterpillar must go through each stage of the transition process in order to transform into a beautiful butterfly, we too must allow Christ to renew, restore and heal us in every area of our lives so that one day we too can become as the butterfly, a beautiful representation of our Lord and Savior Jesus Christ so that all the world can see His glory in and through us!

Today I will take action by:

C.H.A.N.G.E.D.

SCRIPTURE: Matthew 3:8 – "Prove by the way you live that you have repented of your sins and turned to God."

WORD DEFINED: **Changed -** To transform or convert.

IN ACTION: **C**hosen **H**oly **A**nointed **N**ew **G**ifted **E**mpowered & **D**estined

KEY WORDS:
Chosen - preferred; elect;
Holy - having a spiritually pure quality
Anointed - dedicated to the service of God
New - different from the former or the old
Gifted - having great talent or ability
Empowered - to give power or authority to; to authorize
Destined - ordained, appointed, or predetermined to be or do something

FOOD 4 THOUGHT:
John the Baptist called people to more than words or ritual; he told them to change their behavior. "Produce fruit in keeping with repentance" means that God looks beyond our words and religious activities to see if our conduct backs up what we say, and he judges our words by the actions that accompany them. We work hard to keep our outward appearance attractive, but what is in our hearts is even more important. The way we are deep down (where others can't see) matters much to God. When people become Christians, God makes them different on the inside. He will continue the process of change inside them if they only ask. God wants us to seek healthy thoughts and motives, not just healthy food and exercise. True faith transforms our conduct as well as our thoughts. If our lives remain unchanged, we don't truly believe the truths we claim to believe. We

cannot earn our salvation by serving and obeying God. But such actions show that our commitment to God is real.

TAKE ACTION!

What motivates your faith — fear of the future, or a desire to be a better person in a better world? Some people wanted to be baptized by John so they could escape eternal punishment, but they didn't turn to God for salvation. John had harsh words for such people. He knew that God values reformation above ritual. Is your faith motivated by a desire for a new, changed life, or is it only like a vaccination or insurance policy against possible disaster?

Today I will take action by:

C.L.A.S.S.

<u>SCRIPTURE:</u> Psalms 25:21 – "Let integrity and uprightness preserve me, for I wait for you."

<u>WORD DEFINED:</u> Class - Elegance, grace, or dignity, as in dress and behavior.

<u>IN ACTION:</u> **C**haracter **L**eadership **A**ccountability **S**elf-esteem & **S**pirituality

<u>KEY WORDS:</u>

<u>Character</u> - qualities of honesty, courage, or the like
<u>Accountability</u> - responsible; answerable.
<u>Self-esteem</u> - a realistic respect for or favorable impression of oneself
<u>Spirituality</u> - of or pertaining to sacred things or matters; religious; devotional; sacred

<u>FOOD 4 THOUGHT:</u>

When we speak of character I'm specifically referring to "godly" character. Godly character is only produced through the fruit of the spirit (Galatians 5:22-23). No one can dispute the quality of those types of values. There are also some other qualities that are woven into godly character, such as courage, trustfulness, perseverance, honesty, loyalty, reliability, responsibility, integrity, holiness, purity, righteousness, respectfulness, generosity, justice, compassion, integrity, mercifulness, self-sacrifice, wisdom, humility, and endurance to name a few!

Personality and character are not one in the same. One can possess remarkable charm, powerful leadership skills, and spiritual gifts, but have bad character. You must possess godly, mature character in order to stand firm spiritually, because character is what will keep you balanced through everything that happens in your life.

TAKE ACTION:

Ask the Lord to help you to operate in the fullness of godly Character so that you can be a strong Accountable Leader, have positive Self-esteem by knowing and being confident in whom you are in Christ, and possess Spirituality that is alive and active operating in the Fruit of the Spirit! **Now that's CLASS!**

Today I will take action by:

C.P.R.

SCRIPTURE: John 10:10 – "…I have come that they may have life, and have it more abundantly."

WORD DEFINED: CPR – Abbreviation for cardiopulmonary resuscitation, an emergency procedure for reviving heart and lung function.

IN ACTION: **C**hrist's **P**urposed **R**edemption

KEY WORDS:
Purposed- the reason for which something exists or is done, made, used, etc.
Redemption - deliverance; rescue; atonement from guilt.

FOOD 4 THOUGHT:
Many people spend all their energy seeking pleasure. Jesus said, however, that a world of pleasure centered on possessions, position, or power is ultimately worthless. Whatever you have on earth is only temporary; it cannot be exchanged for your soul. If you work hard at getting what you want, you might eventually have a "pleasurable" life, but in the end you will find it hollow and empty. Follow Jesus, and you will know what it means to live abundantly now and to have eternal life as well.

TAKE ACTION:

In contrast to the thief who takes life, Jesus gives life. The life he gives right now is abundantly richer and fuller. It is eternal, yet it begins immediately. Life in Christ is lived on a higher plane because of his overflowing forgiveness, love, and guidance. Have you taken Christ's offer of life? Are you willing to make the pursuit of God more important than the selfish pursuit of pleasure?

Today I will take action by:

D.I.S.C.E.R.N.

SCRIPTURE: Philippians 1:9 - And this is my prayer: that your love may abound more and more in knowledge and depth of insight...

WORD DEFINED: **Discern** - To perceive with the eyes or intellect; detect.

IN ACTION: **D**istinctly **I**nclined to **S**eek **C**hrist in **E**verything **R**efusing to **N**egate

KEY WORDS:
Distinctly - readily and unmistakably
Inclined - drawn toward an opinion or course of conduct
Seek – To inquire for; request
Refuse - To indicate unwillingness to do, accept, give, or allow
Negate - to deny the existence or truth of

FOOD 4 THOUGHT:
Prove [discern/test] all things; hold fast that which is good. Abstain from all appearance of evil (1 Thes.5:21-22). Then it is up to each individual Christian to read their own Bible and be a discerning Christian. The Christian believer must seek the Lord in Spirit and in Truth. If we fail to heed the commands of Scripture, we have no one to blame but ourselves. Let us not forget the words of our Lord Jesus who said, ..."Take heed (discern) that no one deceives you. For many will come in My name, saying, 'I am He,' and will deceive many" (Mark 13:5-6).

TAKE ACTION:

So let us get to work my brothers and sisters in Christ! Let us read our Bibles daily! Let us press on to know Christ and Him crucified! Let us partake of the meat of the Word and mature in the faith! And let us by all means "contend earnestly for the faith which was once [for all] delivered to the saints" (Jude 3). These things please the LORD and these things are part of the normal Christian life. According to the Word; *"Everyone who partakes only of milk is unskilled in the word of righteousness, for he is a babe. But solid food belongs to those who are of full age, that is, those who by reason of use have their senses exercised to discern both good and evil. - Hebrews 5:13-15*

Today I will take action by:

____
____
____
____
____
____
____
____
____
____
____
____
____
____
____
____
____
____
____

D.I.V.A.

SCRIPTURE: Judges 4:4 – "Now Deborah, a prophetess… was judging Israel at that time."

WORD DEFINED: Diva – A distinguished female singer.

IN ACTION: Destined Intrinsic Valued & Anointed

KEY WORDS:
Destined- ordained, appointed, or predetermined to be or do something
Intrinsic - belonging to a thing by its very nature
Valued - highly regarded or esteemed
Anointed - to dedicate to the service of God

FOOD 4 THOUGHT:
The Bible records several women who held national leadership positions, and Deborah was an exceptional woman. Obviously she was the best person for the job, and God chose her to lead Israel. She was in fact a true DIVA!

Wise leaders are rare. They accomplish great amounts of work without direct involvement because they know how to work through other people. They are able to see the big picture that often escapes those directly involved, so they make good mediators, advisers, and planners. Deborah fit this description perfectly. She had all these leadership skills, and she had a remarkable relationship with God. The insight and confidence God gave this woman placed her in a unique position in the Old Testament. Deborah is among the outstanding women of history.

TAKE ACTION:

Deborah's life challenges us in several ways. She reminds us of the need to be available both to God and to others. She encourages us to spend our efforts on what we can do rather than on worrying about what we can't do. Deborah challenges us to be wise leaders. She demonstrates what a person can accomplish when God is in control.

Today I will take action by:

D.O.P.E.

SCRIPTURE: Jeremiah 29:11 – "For I know the plans I have for you, declares the Lord, plans to prosper you and not to harm you, plans to give you hope and a future."

WORD DEFINED: Dope – A word that describes something that is extremely cool, such as music, clothes, people, etc.

IN ACTION: **D**estined **O**rdained **P**urposed & **E**mpowered

KEY WORDS:
Destined- appointed, or predetermined to be or do something
Ordained - (of God) to destine or predestine
Purposed- the reason for which something exists or is done, made, used, etc.
Empower- to give power or authority to; to authorize

FOOD 4 THOUGHT:
God wants your whole life, so he can make something extraordinary out of it. Jesus told his followers, "The thief's purpose is to steal and kill and destroy. My purpose is to give life in all its fullness" (John 10:10). The Christian life was never meant to be done halfway. You're either sold out to God or sold out to the world. For God to give you "abundant life," you must give your life in full to God. Jesus said, "If you cling to your life, you will lose it; but if you give it up for me, you will find it" (Matthew 10:39). And don't worry about what God will ask of you. If he asks you to be a missionary, in effect he is saying; "I know you better than anyone else does. I made you, and I love you more than you'll ever know. Because I put you together, I know what it will take to make you the happiest and most fulfilled in life. If you choose any other direction, you'll be settling for second best.

TAKE ACTION:

We're all encouraged by a leader who stirs us to move ahead, someone who believes we can do the task he has given and who will be with us all the way. God is that kind of leader. He knows the future, and his plans for us are good and full of hope. As long as God, who knows the future, provides our agenda and goes with us as we fulfill his mission, we can have boundless hope. This does not mean that we will be spared pain, suffering, or hardship, but that God will see us through to a glorious conclusion. Now that's DOPE!

Today I will take action by:

F.A.I.T.H.

SCRIPTURE: Hebrews 11:1 – "Faith is the confidence that what we hope for will actually happen; it gives us assurance about things we cannot see."

WORD DEFINED: **Faith –** Confident belief in the truth, value, or trustworthiness of a person, idea, or thing; belief that does not rest on logical proof or material evidence.

IN ACTION: **F**orfeiting **A**ll **I**nhibitions **T**rusting **H**im

KEY WORDS:
Forfeit- to lose or give-up
Inhibition - to restrain, hinder
Trust: to rely on the integrity, strength, and ability of (God)
Him- God

FOOD 4 THOUGHT:
Abram was one of great faith. God told him to leave the comfort of everything he'd always known to go to a foreign place. Abram's response was one of faith, he chose to step out and step up to God's calling. He traveled to new territory at the age of 75 with God as his guide!

There are times when God calls us out of our comfort zone into the unknown which stretches our faith and increases our dependence upon Him. Stepping out in faith may look different for each of us. It may involve reaching out to someone who is lonely or starting an outreach project within the community or church. One thing you can be sure of; as you hear God's call and step out in faith, He will be with you every step of the way and see you through.

TAKE ACTION:

Two words describe faith: *sure* and *certain.* These two qualities need a secure beginning and ending point. The beginning point of faith is believing in God's character — He *is* who He says. The end point is believing in God's promises — He will *do* what He says. When we believe that God will fulfill His promises even though we don't see those promises materializing yet, we demonstrate true faith.

Today I will take action by:

F.I.R.E.

SCRIPTURE: Luke 4:18 – "The Spirit of the LORD is upon me, for he has anointed me to bring Good News..."

WORD DEFINED: Fire - burning passion

IN ACTION: **F**aith **I**gnited **R**estraints **E**xpired

KEY WORDS:
Faith - belief and trust in and loyalty to God
Ignited - to set in motion
Restraints - a control over the expression of one's emotions or thoughts
Expired - to come to an end

FOOD 4 THOUGHT:
In looking back over my life, I have long known a specific purpose that Christ called me too. However, I allowed my fear of failure, rejection and inadequacy to keep me bound and in doing that I failed to have faith that God would provide all I needed. When I began to develop a more intimate relationship with the Lord and allowed Him to bring me into all that He has for me to accomplish here on earth, a passion has began to rise up from deep within my soul. That passion relies on faith not in my abilities but in the ability of an Almighty Savior who has endowed me with power to do all that He has called me to. As that fire has begin to burn inside, it has began to set in motion/ignite a boldness that enables me to begin to walk in the call by exercising the gifts that have been inspired by the Holy Spirit.

TAKE ACTION:

If you've been limited in your ability to move forward into the call God has on your life, I pray that you will now release all those things that hinder you and move forward in faith trusting that God's got you! What we fail to realize is that when God has called you to a specific ministry, it is not you who are operating but you should rely totally upon the Holy Spirit to lead and guide you every step of the way. Faith set in motion (ignited) breaks/brings to an end (expires) the fears (restraints) that have held you back from moving forward into all that God has for your life.

Today I will take action by:

F.L.A.W.E.D.

SCRIPTURE: Matthew 5:48 – "Therefore you shall be perfect, just as your Father in heaven is perfect."

WORD DEFINED: **Flaw** - (used as a verb) a defect; imperfection; weakness; one that detracts from the whole or hinders effectiveness.

IN ACTION: **F**avored, **L**oved, **A**ccepted, **W**hole, **E**mpowered, & **D**estined

KEY WORDS:
Favored - endowed with special advantages or GIFTS
Whole - free of defect or impairment
Empowered - to promote the self-actualization or influence of
Destined - to designate, assign, or dedicate in advance

FOOD 4 THOUGHT: How can we be perfect? (1) *In character.* In this life we cannot be flawless, but we can aspire to be as much like Christ as possible. (2) *In holiness.* Like the Pharisees, we are to separate ourselves from the world's sinful values. But unlike the Pharisees, we are to be devoted to God's desires rather than our own, and carry his love and mercy into the world. (3) *In maturity.* We can't achieve Christ like character and holy living all at once, but we must grow toward maturity and wholeness. Just as we expect different behavior from a baby, a child, a teenager, and an adult, so God expects different behavior from us, depending on our stage of spiritual development. (4) *In love.* We can seek to love others as completely as God loves us.

TAKE ACTION:

We can be perfect if our behavior is appropriate for our maturity level — perfect, yet with much room to grow. Our tendency to sin must never deter us from striving to be more like Christ. Christ calls all of his disciples to excel, to rise above mediocrity, and to mature in every area, becoming like him. Those who strive to become perfect will one day be perfect, even as Christ is perfect (1John 3:2,3).

Today I will take action by:

F.R.E.E.

<u>SCRIPTURE:</u> Psalm 62:5 - "My soul, wait silently for God alone, For my expectation is from Him."

<u>WORD DEFINED:</u> **Free** - Enjoying personal rights or liberty.

<u>IN ACTION:</u> F.R.E.E. - **F**earlessly **R**elinquishing **E**very **E**xpectation

<u>KEY WORDS:</u>
<u>Fearlessly</u> - Without fear; brave
<u>Relinquishing</u> - to give over possession or control of; surrender.
<u>Every</u> - every bit, in every respect; completely
<u>Expectation</u> - to anticipate or look forward to the coming or occurrence of.

<u>FOOD 4 THOUGHT:</u>
Christ desires all of His children to experience being FREE in Him so that we can be effective in the work He has set for us to do. When we allow strongholds to keep us bound we are no longer FREE to do His work. When we realize that our expectations should not be of man but God, the only one who is able to control the heart and mind of man; then and only then can we begin to truly experience being FREE!

You've got a race to run! Hebrews 12:1 - "Wherefore seeing we also are compassed about with so great a cloud of witnesses, let us lay aside every weight, and the sin which doth so easily beset us, and let us run with patience the race that is set before us." Deadweight holds us back so let them go so you can run freely!

TAKE ACTION:

How do you know when it's time to let go? When you're holding on with all your might! Ephesians 6:10 "...be strong in the Lord and in the power of His Might!" Jesus loves you so much... He longs for you to be FREE, He paid your ransom with His life. John 3:16 - He wants you to enjoy the Life He affords you.

Today I will take action by:

G.A.N.G.S.T.A.

SCRIPTURE: I Peter 3:8 – "Finally, all of you be of one mind, having compassion for one another; love as brothers, be tenderhearted, be courteous..."

WORD DEFINED: **Gangsta** - A member of a gang.

IN ACTION: G.A.N.G.S.T.A. – **G**odly **A**bundant **N**ew **G**ifted **S**ecure **T**ransformed & **A**nointed

KEY WORDS:

Abundant – present in great quantity; more than adequate; over sufficient
Gifted – having great special talent or ability
Secure – free from care; without anxiety
Transformed – to change in form, appearance, or structure
Anointed - to dedicate to the service of God

FOOD 4 THOUGHT:

Peter lists five key elements that should characterize any group of believers: (1) harmony — pursuing the same goals; (2) sympathy — being responsive to others' needs; (3) love — seeing and treating each other as brothers and sisters; (4) compassion — being affectionately sensitive and caring; and (5) humility — being willing to encourage one another and rejoice in each other's successes. These five qualities go a long way toward helping believers serve God effectively.

Peter developed the qualities of compassion and humility the hard way. In his early days with Christ, these attitudes did not come naturally to his impulsive, strong-willed personality. But the Holy Spirit changed Peter, molding his strong personality to God's use, and teaching him tenderness and humility. In our fallen world, it is often deemed acceptable by some to tear people down verbally or to get back at them if we feel hurt. Peter, remembering Jesus' teaching to turn the other cheek, encourages his readers to pay back wrongs by praying for the offenders.

TAKE ACTION

In God's kingdom, revenge is unacceptable behavior, as is insulting a person, no matter how indirectly it is done. Rise above getting back at those who hurt you. Instead of reacting angrily to these people, pray for them.

Today I will take action by:

G.E.M.S.

SCRIPTURE: Matthew 10:31 – "Do not fear therefore; you are of more value than many sparrows."

WORD DEFINED: **Gems** - jewel *b* **:** a precious or sometimes semiprecious stone cut and polished for ornament; something prized especially for great beauty or perfection

IN ACTION: **G.E.M.S.** – **G**od **E**mpowered and **M**otivated to **S**ucceed

KEY WORDS:

Empowered- to give power or authority to

Motivated – to provide with a reason to act in a certain way; incentive

Succeed - something that incites or tends to incite to action or greater effort, as a reward offered for increased productivity

FOOD 4 THOUGHT:

Jesus said that God cares for the sparrows' every need. We are far more valuable to God than these little birds, so valuable that God sent his only Son to die for us (John 3:16). You are of great worth to God. Because he places such value on you, you need never fear personal threats or difficult trials. But don't think that because you are valuable to God he will take away all your troubles (see 10:16). The real test of value is how well something holds up under the wear, tear, and abuse of everyday life. Those who stand up for Christ in spite of their troubles truly have lasting value and will receive great rewards (see 5:11-12).

TAKE ACTION

The real value of a person is inside, not outside. Although a person's body may be diseased or deformed, the person inside is no less valuable to God. No person is too disgusting for God's touch. In a sense, we are all people with leprosy because we have all been deformed by the ugliness of sin. But God, by sending his Son Jesus, has touched us, giving us the opportunity to be healed. When you feel repulsed by someone, stop and remember how God feels about that person — and about you.

Today I will take action by:

G.H.E.T.T.O.

SCRIPTURE: I Peter 2:9 - But you are not like that, for you are a **chosen** people. You are royal priests, a holy nation, God's very own possession. As a result, you can show others the goodness of God, for he called you out of the darkness into his wonderful light.

WORD DEFINED: **Ghetto** - section of a city, esp. a thickly populated slum (run down) area, inhabited predominantly by members of an ethnic or other minority group, often as a result of social or economic restrictions, pressures, or hardships (poor people)

IN ACTION: **G**ifted **H**oly **E**mpowered **T**ransformed **T**riumphant & **O**rdained

KEY WORDS:
Gifted - having great special talent or ability
Holy - dedicated or devoted to the service of God
Empowered - to give power or authority to; to enable or permit
Transformed - to change in condition, nature, or character; convert
Triumphant - having achieved victory or success; victorious; successful
Ordained - to destine or predestine

FOOD 4 THOUGHT:
In the Gospel of John, Nathaniel asks, "Can anything good come out of Nazareth?" *(John 1:46)* The meaning of this cryptic question is debated. Some commentators and scholars suggest that it means Nazareth was very small and unimportant, but the question does not speak of Nazareth's size but of its goodness. In fact, Nazareth was described negatively by the evangelists; the Gospel of Mark argues that Nazareth did not believe in Jesus and therefore he could "do no mighty work there", *(Mark 6:5)*; in the Gospel of Luke, the Nazarenes

are portrayed as attempting to kill Jesus by throwing him off a cliff; *(Luke 4:29). One could* conclude that based on this information Jesus lived in a ghetto.

<u>TAKE ACTION:</u>

In God's eyes, a person's value has no relationship to his or her wealth or position on the social ladder. Many people who have excelled in God's work began in poverty or humble beginnings. God supersedes the social orders of this world, often choosing his future leaders and ambassadors from among social outcasts. Do you treat the unwanted in society as though they have value? Demonstrate by your actions that all people are valuable and useful in God's eyes.

Today I will take action by:

G.I.A.N.T.S.

SCRIPTURE: I Samuel 17:46 – "...For who is this uncircumcised Philistine, that he should defy the armies of the living God."

WORD DEFINED: **Giant -** Unusually large, great, or strong.

IN ACTION: **G**od **I**ntended **A**ction to **N**urturing **T**rust & **S**trength

KEY WORDS:

Intended - to have in mind as a purpose or goal
Action - the accomplishment of a thing usually over a period of time
Nurture - something that nourishes
Trust – assured reliance on the character, ability, strength, or truth of someone or something
Strength– the quality or state of being strong : capacity for exertion or endurance

FOOD 4 THOUGHT:

When the giant criticized, insulted and threatened, David didn't stop or even waver. Everyone else cowered in fear, but David ran to the battle. He knew that action needed to be taken. David did the right thing in spite of discouraging insults and fearful threats. Only God's opinion mattered to David. David's faith in God caused him to look at the giant from a different perspective. Goliath was merely a mortal man defying an all-powerful God. David looked at the battle from God's point of view. If we look at giant problems and impossible situations from God's perspective, we realize that God will fight for us and with us. When we put things in proper perspective, we see more clearly and we can fight more effectively.

TAKE ACTION

At some point in each of our lives we are faced with what we term as "giants"/difficult situations. It is at this moment as Christians that the test of our faith is made manifest. It is at these defining moments, in the heat of battle, that our faith and dependence on Christ is tested. My brothers and sisters, take comfort in knowing that nothing comes your way without God allowing it in order to bring about His glory and build your faith and trust in Him. (Reference: Job's life in the book of Job)

Always remember, no matter how small or large the giant in your life may seem, you serve a God who is able to do exceedingly, abundantly, above all you could ever think or imagine! **Even GIANTS must fall down and bow at the NAME of Jesus!**

Today I will take action by:

____

G.L.E.A.N.

SCRIPTURE: Ruth 2:23 – "So **she kept fast** by the maidens of Boaz to **glean unto the end** of barley **harvest** and of wheat harvest; and **dwelt** with her mother in law."

WORD DEFINED: **Glean** - to gather; pick-up; grain or other produce left by reapers.

IN ACTION: **G**odly **L**oyal **E**arnest **A**bstinent **N**urturing

KEY WORDS:

Godly – conforming to the laws and wishes of God
Loyal – faithful to one's oath, commitments, or obligations: *to be loyal to a vow.*
Earnest – serious in intention, purpose, or effort; sincerely zealous: *an earnest worker.*
Abstinent - self-restraint, self-denial
Nurturing - to support and encourage, as during the period of training or development; foster:

FOOD 4 THOUGHT:

In reading Ruth 1:16-17 the following characteristics of Ruth are noted: she was godly and abstinent, only a person with a heart for Christ would make such a selfless sacrifice as Ruth did in choosing to deny her own desires and leave her home land to go into a foreign country to be with her windowed, elderly and poor mother-in-law. She proved to be loyal because she kept her vow to stay with her no matter what. She proved to be earnest/sincere by asking the Lord to punish her if she did not keep her vow. Her nurturing spirit was evidenced by her willingness to care for Naomi by gleaning in the field to provide for her. What Ruth didn't realize was that as she gleaned in the fields, not only was she noticed by Boaz the owner, but God also took notice of her faithfulness, obedience, loyalty, earnest intentions, self-denial and nurturing spirit. As she was busy picking up leftovers from the harvest of others, God was preparing a harvest of His own just for her!

<u>TAKE ACTION</u>

Ruth's life exhibited admirable qualities and they gained for her a good reputation, but only because she displayed them *consistently* in all areas of her life. Wherever Ruth went or whatever she did, her character remained the same. Your reputation is formed by the people who watch you at work, in town, at home, in church. A good reputation comes by *consistently* living out the qualities you believe in no matter what group of people or surroundings you are in.

Today I will take action by:

G.R.A.C.E.

SCRIPTURE: 2 Corinthians 12:9 - "...My grace is sufficient for you, for My strength is made perfect in weakness." Therefore most gladly I will rather boast in my infirmities, that the power of Christ may rest upon me."

WORD DEFINED: **Grace** - God's love in action towards men who merited the opposite of love. "Unmerited favor" from God. It is the outpouring of the love of God on humanity.

IN ACTION: **G**od's **R**edemption **A**nd **C**are **E**xercised

KEY WORDS:
Redemption - To set free; rescue or ransom.
Care - Attentive assistance or treatment to those in need
Exercised - An act of employing or putting into play; use

FOOD 4 THOUGHT:
God's grace is something we cannot earn, or repay; it is through His love and concern for us that He continually bestows what is needed to make it through life in spite of what we are faced with. As the apostle Paul experienced a piercing/uneasiness (see vs. 7-8 also) which is referred to as a thorn in his flesh; we too experience uneasiness in our lives, we refer to these as trials/difficult times. In the word we are also admonished not think strangely when we are faced with trials and difficulties (I Peter 4:12-13), for through them we are strengthened and grow into the men and women God has ordained us to be. We are not to lose hope or become depressed; instead we are told to rejoice! Then how is it possible to rejoice when all hell is breaking loose around you? It is only when we submit to the Lord, focus our attention towards Him and allow the Holy Spirit to indwell us with the strength needed to endure, trusting that God is in

control of every situation we face and thus claiming that "His grace is sufficient/more than enough to see us through.

TAKE ACTION

Grace is God's voluntary and loving favor given to those he saves. We can't earn salvation, nor do we deserve it. No religious, intellectual, or moral effort can gain it, because it comes only from God's mercy and love. Without God's grace, no person can be saved. To receive it, we must acknowledge that we cannot save ourselves, that only God can save us, and that our only way to receive this loving favor is through faith in Christ.

Today I will take action by:

H.Y.P.E.

SCRIPTURE: James 4:6 - "...God opposes the proud, but gives grace to the humble."

WORD DEFINED: Hype – To stimulate, excite, or agitate.

IN ACTION: **H**umble **Y**ielded **P**urposed **&** **E**mpowered

KEY WORDS:

Humble - marked by meekness or modesty in behavior, attitude, or spirit; not arrogant or prideful.

Yielded - to give up possession of on claim or demand
Purposed - to propose as an aim
Empowered - to promote the self-actualization or influence of

FOOD 4 THOUGHT:

How can we humble ourselves? Some people try to give the appearance of humility in order to manipulate others. Others think that humility means putting themselves down. Truly humble people compare themselves only with Christ, realize their sinfulness, and understand their limitations. On the other hand, they also recognize their gifts and strengths and are willing to use them as Christ directs. Humility is not self-degradation; it is realistic assessment and commitment to serve. Being humble involves having a true perspective about ourselves (see Romans 12:3). Before God, we are sinners, saved only by God's grace, but we *are* saved and therefore have great worth in God's kingdom. We are to lay aside selfishness and treat others with respect and common courtesy. Considering others' interests as more important than our own links us with Christ, who was a true example of humility.

TAKE ACTION

The cure for evil desires is humility. Pride makes us self-centered and leads us to conclude that we deserve all we can see, touch, or imagine. It creates greedy appetites for far more than we need. We can be released from our self-centered desires by humbling ourselves before God, realizing that all we really need is his approval. When the Holy Spirit fills us, we see that this world's seductive attractions are only cheap substitutes for what God has to offer.

Today I will take action by:

J.O.Y.

SCRIPTURE: Philippians 4:4 - "Rejoice in the Lord always. Again I say rejoice!"

WORD DEFINED: **Joy** – A source or cause of keen pleasure or delight.

IN ACTION: **J**esus **O**utpouring in **Y**ou

KEY WORDS:
Outpouring - a passionate or exaggerated outburst!

FOOD 4 THOUGHT:
It seems strange that a man in prison would be telling a church to rejoice. But Paul's attitude teaches us an important lesson: our inner attitudes do not have to reflect our outward circumstances. Paul was full of joy because he knew that no matter what happened to him, Jesus Christ was with him. Several times in this letter, Paul urged the Philippians to be joyful, probably because they needed to hear this. It's easy to get discouraged about unpleasant circumstances or to take unimportant events too seriously. If you haven't been joyful lately, you may not be looking at life from the right perspective. Ultimate joy comes from Christ dwelling within us. Christ is near, and at his second coming we will fully realize this ultimate joy. He who lives within us will fulfill his final purposes for us.

TAKE ACTION

Unlike happiness which is dependant upon favorable external circumstances, JOY is a Gift from God which enables believers to find hope and peace even in unfavorable circumstances. Consider your response to both good and bad times. Does a consistent joy in Christ give you strength? Or do you find emotional relief only in the midst of positive circumstances? Difficulty is inevitable but God's truth is able to sustain you. Rely on Him for emotional security.

Today I will take action by:

J.U.S.T.I.F.I.E.D.

SCRIPTURE: Romans 5:1-2 - "Being therefore justified by faith, we have peace with God through our Lord Jesus Christ; through whom also we have had our access by faith into this grace wherein we stand; and we rejoice in hope of the glory of God."

WORD DEFINED: **Justified** – To declare innocent or guiltless; absolve; acquit.

IN ACTION: **J**esus **U**ltimate **S**acrifice **T**o **I**ndemnify **F**aults **I**nhibiting **E**ternal **D**amnation

KEY WORDS:

Ultimate - Utmost; extreme

Sacrifice - A loss so sustained; to give up for something or someone else.

Indemnify - To protect against damage, loss, or injury; insure.

Inhibiting - to forbid

Eternal - without beginning or end; lasting forever; always existing

Damnation - condemnation to eternal punishment as a consequence of sin

FOOD 4 THOUGHT:

Paul states that, as believers, we now stand in a place of highest privilege ("this grace in which we now stand"). Not only has God declared us not guilty; he has drawn us close to himself. Instead of being enemies, we have become his friends — in fact, his own children (John 15:15; Galatians 4:5). We now have peace *with God,* which may differ from peaceful feelings such as calmness and tranquility. Peace with God means that we have been reconciled with him. There is no more hostility between us, no sin blocking our relationship with him. Peace with God is possible only because Jesus paid the price for our sins through his death on the cross.

TAKE ACTION:

As Paul states clearly in 1Corinthians 13:13, faith, hope, and love are at the heart of the Christian life. Our relationship with God begins with *faith,* which helps us realize that we are delivered from our past by Christ's death. *Hope* grows as we learn all that God has in mind for us; it gives us the promise of the future. And God's *love* fills our lives and gives us the ability to reach out to others.

Today I will take action by:

L.E.A.D.E.R.

SCRIPTURE : I Peter 5:3 – "Do not lord it over the people entrusted to you, but be examples to the flock."

WORD DEFINED: **Leader** – A guiding or directing head as in a movement, army, or other group.

IN ACTION: : **L**oyal **E**ntrusted **A**nointed **D**estined **E**mpowered & **R**ighteous

KEY WORDS:

Loyal - – faithful to one's oath, commitments, or obligations: *to be loyal to a vow.*

Entrusted – to charge or invest with a trust or responsibility

Anointed – to dedicate to the service of God

Destined – ordained, appointed, or predetermined to be or do something

Empowered – to give power or authority to; to enable or permit

Righteous - characterized by uprightness or morality

FOOD 4 THOUGHT:

God chooses His leaders. Moses didn't go out looking to be a leader. He tried every way to get out of it. *"The gifts and calling of God are without repentance."* (Romans 11:29. If a person wants to be a leader, he or she needs to realize that many peoples' favorite game is "Hate the Leader." Some will hate you simply because you are the leader.

- Leadership is chosen by God, not by those who are seeking an office.
- Leadership brings awesome responsibility and is not to be entered into lightly!
- Leaders will be judged by the Ultimate Leader – Jesus Christ.

TAKE ACTION:

God's promise to supernaturally equip the leader. Numbers 11:17 *"And I (God) will come down and talk wit thee there: and I will take of the spirit which is upon thee, and will put it upon them; and they shall bear the burden of the people with thee, that thou bear it not thyself alone."* This means each leader that God calls will be given the anointed help that he or she needs, just like Moses was. God can choose anyone to lead his people, young or old, man or woman. Don't let your prejudices get in the way of those God may have chosen to lead you.

Today I will take action by:

L.I.F.E.

SCRIPTURE: Matthew 10:39 – "He that findeth his life shall lose it: and he that loseth his life for my sake shall find it."

WORD DEFINED: **Life** - A corresponding state, existence, or principle of existence conceived of as belonging to the soul.

IN ACTION: **L**ove **I**nspiration **F**aith & **E**mpowerment

KEY WORDS:
Love - affectionate concern for the well-being of others
Inspire - to influence or impel
Faith - belief that is not based on proof
Empowerment - to give power or authority to; to authorize

FOOD 4 THOUGHT:
This verse is a positive and negative statement of the same truth: clinging to this life may cause us to forfeit the best from Christ in this world *and* in the next. The more we love this life's rewards (leisure, power, popularity, financial security), the more we will discover how empty they really are. The best way to enjoy life, therefore, is to loosen our greedy grasp on earthly rewards so that we can be free to follow Christ. In doing so, we will inherit eternal life and begin at once to experience the benefits of following Christ.

TAKE ACTION:

All who welcome Jesus Christ as Lord of their lives are reborn spiritually, receiving new life from God. Through faith in Christ, this new birth changes us from the inside out — rearranging our attitudes, desires, and motives. Being born of God makes you spiritually alive and puts you in God's family (John 1:12). Have you asked Christ to make you a new person? This fresh start in life is available to all who believe in Christ.

Today I will take action by:

L.I.G.H.T.

SCRIPTURE: Ephesians 5:8 – “For you were once darkness, but now you are light in the Lord. Live as children of light.”

WORD DEFINED: Light – something that makes things visible or affords illumination; an illuminating agent or source, as the sun, a lamp, or a beacon.

IN ACTION: **L**iving **I**n **G**od’s **H**oliness & **T**ruth

KEY WORDS:

Living – in actual existence or use
Holiness – dedicated or devoted to the service of God
Truth - an obvious or accepted fact

FOOD 4 THOUGHT:

If we live for Christ, we will glow like lights, showing others what Christ is like. We hide our light by (1) being quiet when we should speak, (2) going along with the crowd, (3) denying the light, (4) letting sin dim our light, (5) not explaining our light to others, or (6) ignoring the needs of others. Be a beacon of truth — don't shut your light off from the rest of the world. The light of Jesus' truth is revealed to us, not hidden. But we may not be able to see or to use all of that truth right now. Only as we put God's teachings into practice will we understand and see more of the truth. The truth is clear, but our ability to understand is imperfect. As we obey, we will sharpen our vision and increase our understanding.

TAKE ACTION:

If a lamp doesn't help people see, it is useless. Does your life show other people how to find God and how to live for him? If not, ask what "bowls" have extinguished your light. Complacency, resentment, stubbornness of heart, or disobedience could keep God's light from shining through you to others.

Today I will take action by:

O.B.E.Y.

SCRIPTURE: I Peter 1:14 – *"As obedient children, do not conform to the evil desires you had when you lived in ignorance."*

WORD DEFINED: **Obey** - To carry out or fulfill the command, order, or instruction of.

IN ACTION: **O**peratively **B**eing an **E**xample of **Y**ielding

KEY WORDS:
Operatively – Functioning effectively; efficient
Example – One serving as a pattern of a specific kind
Yielding - To give over possession of, as in deference; surrender

FOOD 4 THOUGHT:
Obedience is what is required of the Christian (I Peter 1:14-15). Obedience is compliance to the plan; conformity to the pattern; observance of the rules; adherence to the standard; and submission to the will of the Lord. In order to be obedient to the Lord it is necessary to know what He requires of you. How do you find out what He requires you ask? By reading and meditating upon the Word. ....they parish for lack of knowledge (Hosea 4:6).

Just like playing a game of monopoly or any other board or electronic game, if you don't read the manual you break all kinds of rules and thus the game does not turn out the way it should have; the end results are altered. That's just the same with our Christian walk, if we are not in the word and a relationship with the Lord, we end up somewhere off course, away from our intended purpose and plan, all because we did not obey the instructions. We must also realize that the Promises of God are all conditional upon our obedience to His Word. If we do not walk according to the Word then we will miss out on His promises.

TAKE ACTION:

Once you begin reading the word then comes knowledge of what is expected of you, therefore you begin to conform to it; in other words obey it. You may ask how can I possibly keep all the commandments in the Bible… well, I have good news for you, you can't, but the Holy Spirit is able to help you do all things. Christ left the Holy Spirit as our helper (John 14:15-17).

Today I will take action by:

P.E.A.C.E.

SCRIPTURE: Philippians 4:7 – “And God's peace which transcends all understanding shall [b]garrison and mount guard over your hearts and minds in Christ Jesus.”

WORD DEFINED: **Peace**– Freedom from any strife or dissension.

IN ACTION: **P**urposely **E**ntrusting the **A**lmighty **C**oncerning **E**verything

KEY WORDS:
Purposely – the reason for which something exists or is done
Entrusting – to charge or invest with a trust or responsibility
The Almighty – God; Jesus Christ.

FOOD 4 THOUGHT:
JEHOVAH SHALOM - The Lord our Peace. Experiencing God as Jehovah-Shalom is realizing peace. This is peace that is unlike anything that we know in this world. It is not found in the absence of conflict or in the use of positive thinking. It is beyond our understanding. This is the peace that comes from knowing that God is in control and that we are children of the King, bound for the kingdom. When we accept Jesus as our savior, that peace is ours. However, you may know as well as I do that experiencing it isn’t automatic, we can still hold onto worries and concerns. To know Jehovah-Shalom we have to believe the promises of God.

TAKE ACTION:

Look up the verses below, memorize and meditate on them. They are a good place to start in order to experience Jehovah-Shalom:

- He searches the whole earth to strengthen anyone whose heart is fully committed to Him. He has placed us where He wants us and He will give us the strength to complete the task. 2 Chronicles 16:9
- God will take care of all our needs, both physical and spiritual. Philippians 4:19
- He will use the difficulties in life to help us grow in character. Romans 5:3
- With God's help we will do mighty things. Psalm 60:12

Today I will take action by:

____

____

____

____

____

____

____

____

____

____

____

____

____

____

____

____

____

____

P.H.A.T.

SCRIPTURE: Romans 8:29 – "For whom He foreknew, He also predestined to be conformed to the image of His son…"

WORD DEFINED: **Phat** – Excellent; first-rate.

IN ACTION: **P**redestined **H**oly **A**nointed & **T**riumphant

KEY WORDS:

Predestined – foreordain; predetermine
Holy - having a spiritually pure quality
Anointed – dedicated to the service of God
Triumphant - having achieved victory or success; victorious; successful

FOOD 4 THOUGHT:

Some believe these verses mean that before the beginning of the world, God chose certain people to receive his gift of salvation. They point to verses like Ephesians 1:11 that says we are "predestined according to the plan of him who works out everything in conformity with the purpose of his will." Others believe that God *foreknew* those who would respond to him and upon those he set his mark (predestined). What is clear is that God's *purpose* for people was not an afterthought; it was settled before the foundation of the world. People are to serve and honor God. If you have believed in Christ, you can rejoice in the fact that God has always known you. God's love is eternal. His wisdom and power are supreme. He will guide and protect you until you one day stand in his presence.

TAKE ACTION:

Our "calling" from God, as Christians, is to become like Christ (Romans 8:29). This is a gradual, lifelong process that will be completed when we see Christ face to face (1John 3:2). To be "worthy" of this calling means to *want* to do what is right and good (as Christ would). We aren't perfect yet, but we're moving in that direction as God works in us.

Today I will take action by:

P.O.S.I.T.I.V.E.

SCRIPTURE: Psalm 11:1- In the LORD put I my trust: how say ye to my soul, Flee *as* a bird to your mountain?

WORD DEFINED: Positive - indicating, relating to, or characterized by affirmation, addition, inclusion, or presence rather than negation, withholding, or absence; Characterized by or displaying certainty, acceptance, or affirmation.

IN ACTION: **P**racticing **O**ptimism **S**peaking **I**t **T**hus **I**nspiring **V**ictorious **E**xpectations

KEY WORDS:
Practicing – actively engaged.
Optimism – to anticipate the best possible outcome.
Inspiring – to draw forth or bring out.
Victorious - a sense of fulfillment.
Expectations – anticipating or looking forward to.

FOOD 4 THOUGHT:
David was forced to flee for safety several times. Being God's anointed king did not make him immune to injustice and hatred from others. This psalm may have been written when he was being hunted by Saul (1Samuel 18 — 31) or during the days of Absalom's rebellion (2Samuel 15 — 18). In both instances, David fled, but not as if all was lost. He knew God was in control. While David wisely avoided trouble, he did not fearfully run away from his troubles. Faith in God keeps us from losing hope and helps us resist fear. David was comforted and optimistic because he knew God was greater than anything his enemies could bring against him (Psalms 7:10; 16:1; 31:2,3).

TAKE ACTION:

When the foundations are shaking and you wish you could hide, remember that God is still in control. His power is not diminished by any turn of events. Nothing happens without his knowledge and permission. When you feel like running away — run to God. He will restore justice and goodness on the earth in his good time.

Today I will take action by:

P.O.W.E.R.

SCRIPTURE: Acts 1:8 – "But you will receive power when the Holy Spirit comes upon you…"

WORD DEFINED: **Power** – Great or marked ability to do or act; strength; might; force.

IN ACTION: **P**ressing **O**n **W**ith **E**xtraordinary **R**esilience

KEY WORDS:
Pressing - to follow through; a course of Action.
Extraordinary - going beyond what is usual, regular or customary.
Resilience - to recover from or adjust easily to misfortune or change.

FOOD 4 THOUGHT:
Jesus had instructed his disciples to witness to people of all nations about him (Matthew 28:19,20). But they were told to wait first for the Holy Spirit (Luke 24:49). God has important work for you to do for him, but you must do it by the power of the Holy Spirit. We often like to get on with the job, even if it means running ahead of God. But waiting is sometimes part of God's plan.

This verse describes a series of ever-widening circles. The gospel was to spread, geographically, from Jerusalem, into Judea and Samaria, and finally to the whole world. It would begin with the devout Jews in Jerusalem and Samaria, spread to the mixed race in Samaria, and finally be offered to the Gentiles in the uttermost parts of the earth. God's gospel has not reached its final destination if someone in your family, your workplace, your school, or your community hasn't heard about Jesus Christ. Make sure that you are contributing in some way to the ever-widening circle of God's loving message.

TAKE ACTION:

Are you waiting and listening for God's complete instructions, or are you running ahead of his plans? We need God's timing and power to be truly effective.

Today I will take action by:

P.R.A.I.S.E.

SCRIPTURE: Acts 16:25-26 - "About midnight Paul and Silas were praying and singing hymns to God, and the other prisoners were listening to them. Suddenly there was such a violent earthquake that the foundations of the prison were shaken. At once all the prison doors flew open, and everybody's chains came loose."

WORD DEFINED: Praise - The offering of grateful homage in words or song, as an act of worship.

IN ACTION: **P**ower **R**eleased **A**s **I** **S**hout **E**xuberantly

KEY WORDS:
power - Great or marked ability to do or act; strength; might; force
released - to free from confinement, bondage
exuberantly - joyously unrestrained and enthusiastic

FOOD 4 THOUGHT:
Paul and Silas were stripped, beaten, and placed in stocks in the inner cell. Despite this dismal situation, they praised God, praying and singing as the other prisoners listened. No matter what our circumstances, we should praise God. Others may come to Christ because of our example.

II Chronicles 20:21, 22 - " After consulting the people, Jehoshaphat appointed men to sing to the LORD and to praise him for the splendor of his [d] holiness as they went out at the head of the army, saying:"Give thanks to the LORD, for his love endures forever." [22] As they began to sing and praise, the LORD set ambushes against the men of Ammon and Moab and Mount Seir who were invading Judah, and they were defeated.

TAKE ACTION:

Are you faced with situations or emotions that render you helpless and lacking in faith and hope? I pray that you truly submit to PRAISING the Lord right where you are and see His Salvation come to your rescue! Even though we have our plans and idea of what we'd like God to do in the situation, we must remember He knows what is best and nothing comes your way without Him allowing it. Everything satan attempts to destroy you with has already been filtered through the hands of a loving God, who will not allow nothing to come your way that you have not been equipped to handle.

Today I will take action by:

P.R.E.S.S.

<u>SCRIPTURE:</u> Philippians 3:12-14 – "Not as though I had already attained, either were already perfect; but I follow after, if that I may apprehend that for which also I am apprehended of Christ Jesus. I press toward the mark for the prize of the high calling of God in Christ Jesus."

<u>WORD DEFINED:</u> **Press** – To urge or entreat strongly or insistently.

<u>IN ACTION:</u> **P**ursue **R**elease **E**ngage **S**trive **S**tand

<u>KEY WORDS:</u>
<u>Pursue</u> - to strive to gain; seek to attain or accomplish
<u>Release</u> - to free from confinement, bondage
<u>Engage</u> - to attract and hold fast
<u>Strive</u> - to contend in opposition, battle, or any conflict

<u>FOOD 4 THOUGHT:</u>
Paul had reason to forget what was behind — he had held the coats of those who stoned Stephen, the first Christian martyr (<u>Acts 7:57,58</u>, Paul is called Saul here). We have all done things for which we are ashamed, and we live in the tension of what we have been and what we want to be. Because our hope is in Christ, however, we can let go of past guilt and look forward to what God will help us become. Don't dwell on your past. Instead, grow in the knowledge of God by concentrating on your relationship with him *now.* Realize that you are forgiven, and then move on to a life of faith and obedience. Look forward to a fuller and more meaningful life because of your hope in Christ.

TAKE ACTION:

Paul says that his goal is to know Christ, to be like Christ, and to be all Christ has in mind for him. This goal absorbs all Paul's energy. This is a helpful example for us. We should not let anything take our eyes off our goal — knowing Christ. With the single-mindedness of an athlete in training, we must lay aside everything harmful and forsake anything that may distract us from being effective Christians. What is holding you back?

Today I will take action by:

P.R.U.N.I.N.G.

SCRIPTURE: John 15:2 – "Every branch in me that does not bear fruit He takes away; and every branch that bears fruit He prunes; that it may bear more fruit."

WORD DEFINED: Pruning - To rid or clear of (anything superfluous or undesirable).

IN ACTION: Purging **R**esidual **U**ntil **N**othing **I**nterrupts **N**ewness & **G**rowth

KEY WORDS:
Purge - elimination, removal
Residual - a quantity left over at the end of a process
Interrupt - to disturb or halt an ongoing process or action by interfering suddenly
Growth - the act or process, or a manner of growing; development; gradual increase.

FOOD 4 THOUGHT:
Jesus makes a distinction between two kinds of pruning: (1) separating and (2) cutting back branches. Fruitful branches are cut back to promote growth. In other words, God must sometimes discipline us to strengthen our character and faith. But branches that don't bear fruit are cut off at the trunk because not only are they worthless, but they often infect the rest of the tree. People who won't bear fruit for God or who try to block the efforts of God's followers will be cut off from his life-giving power.

TAKE ACTION:

God tested Abraham (Genesis 22:1), not to trip him and watch him fall, but to deepen his capacity to obey God and thus to develop his character. Just as fire refines ore to extract precious metals, God refines us through difficult circumstances. When we are tested we can complain, or we can try to see how God is stretching us to develop our character.

Today I will take action by:

R.E.J.E.C.T.E.D.

SCRIPTURE: Psalm 118:22 – "The stone which the builders rejected has become the chief cornerstone."

WORD DEFINED: **Rejected** – To discard as useless or unsatisfactory.

IN ACTION: **R**epositioned **E**mpowered **J**ustified **E**quipped **C**alled-out **T**ransformed **E**steemed & **D**estined

KEY WORDS:
Reposition - To place or put in a new position; position again
Empower - To equip or supply with an ability; enable
Justify - To free (a human) of the guilt and penalty attached to sin
Equip - To furnish with the qualities necessary for performance
Called-out - To order or request to undertake a particular activity
Transform - to alter or be altered radically in form, function
Esteemed - to alter or be altered radically in form, function
Destined - To determine beforehand; preordain

FOOD 4 THOUGHT:
Jesus referred to this verse when he spoke of being rejected by his own people. Although he was rejected, Jesus is now the "capstone," the most important part of the church. The capstone is the center stone in the top of an arch, holding the whole arch together.

Rejection comes with being a Christian, because our life and beliefs go against the flow of the rest of the world. Growing closer to God will naturally make you grow further away from the world. Read Acts 7:54-60. Stephen took a stand for Christ that cost him much more than rejection from a few friends. It cost him his life. Read further, and in Acts 8 and 9 you will see what the results of a fearless faith can be.

TAKE ACTION:

People are watching you and other Christians. They are seeing how you respond to rejection and verbal abuse. Within the world there are people who want to believe in something true, something worth living for no matter what the cost. And when they find it, they may make an incredible impact in their world for Christ. What do they learn from watching you?

Today I will take action by:

R.I.C.H.

<u>SCRIPTURE:</u> Psalm 107:2 – "Let the redeemed of the Lord say so, whom He has redeemed from the hand of the enemy."

<u>WORD DEFINED:</u> Rich – Having great worth or value.

<u>IN ACTION:</u> Redeemed **I**n **C**hrist & **H**oly

<u>KEY WORDS:</u>
<u>Redeemed</u> - To set free; rescue or ransom
<u>Holy</u> - Belonging to, derived from, or associated with a divine power; sacred

<u>FOOD 4 THOUGHT:</u>
A ransom was the price paid to release a slave from bondage. Jesus often told his disciples that he must die to redeem all people from the bondage of sin and death. The disciples thought that Jesus could save them as long as he was alive. But Jesus revealed that only his death would save them and the world.

To speak of Jesus' blood was an important first-century way of speaking of Christ's death. His death points to two wonderful truths — redemption and forgiveness. *Redemption* was the price paid to gain freedom for a slave. Through his death, Jesus paid the price to release us from slavery to sin. *Forgiveness* was granted in Old Testament times on the basis of the shedding of animals' blood. Now we are forgiven on the basis of the shedding of Jesus' blood — he died as the perfect and final sacrifice.

TAKE ACTION:

Jesus means "the LORD saves." Jesus came to earth to save us because we can't save ourselves from sin and its consequences. No matter how good we are, we can't eliminate the sinful nature present in all of us. Only Jesus can do that. Jesus didn't come to help people save themselves; he came to be their Savior from the power and penalty of sin. Thank Christ for his death on the cross for your sin, and then ask him to take control of your life. Your new life begins at that moment.

Today I will take action by:

S.O.S.

<u>SCRIPTURE</u>: Ephesians 6:17 – "…and the sword of the spirit, which is the word of God."

<u>WORD DEFINED:</u> SOS – The letters represented by the Morse Code signal; used as an international distress signal, especially by ships and aircraft.

<u>IN ACTION:</u> Swords **O**f the **S**pirit

<u>KEY WORDS:</u>

<u>Sword</u> - An instrument of death or destruction
<u>Spirit</u> - A supernatural being

<u>FOOD 4 THOUGHT:</u>

We are engaged in a spiritual battle - all believers find themselves subject to Satan's attacks because they are no longer on Satan's side. Thus, Paul tells us to use every piece of God's armor to resist Satan's attacks and to stand true to God in the midst of those attacks.

These who are not "flesh and blood" are demons over whom Satan has control. They are not mere fantasies — they are very real. We face a powerful army whose goal is to defeat Christ's church. When we believe in Christ, these beings become our enemies, and they try every device to turn us away from him and back to sin. Although we are assured of victory, we must engage in the struggle until Christ returns, because Satan is constantly battling against all who are on the Lord's side. We need supernatural power to defeat Satan, and God has provided this by giving us his Holy Spirit within us and his armor surrounding us.

TAKE ACTION:

If you feel discouraged, remember Jesus' words to Peter: "On this rock I will build my church, and the gates of Hades will not overcome it" (Matthew 16:18).

The sword is the only weapon of offense in the list of armor. There are times when we need to take the offensive against Satan. When we are tempted, we need to trust in the truth of God's Word.

Today I will take action by:

S.T.E.P.S.

SCRIPTURE: Proverbs 4:12 – "When you walk, your steps will not be hindered, and when you run, you will not stumble."

WORD DEFINED: **Steps** – Course; path.

IN ACTION: **S**ecure **T**riumphant **E**mpowered **P**urposed & **S**ure

KEY WORDS:

Secure - Free from fear, anxiety, or doubt
Triumphant - To be victorious or successful; win
Empowered - To equip or supply with an ability; enable
Purposed - The object toward which one strives or for which something exists; an aim or a goal
Sure - Not hesitating or wavering; firm

FOOD 4 THOUGHT:

God doesn't always work in the way that seems best to us. Instead of guiding the Israelites along the direct route from Egypt to the promised land, he took them by a longer route to avoid fighting with the Philistines (Exodus 13:17). If God does not lead you along the shortest path to your goal, don't complain or resist. Follow him willingly and trust him to lead you safely around unseen obstacles. He can see the end of your journey from the beginning, and he knows the safest and best route.

TAKE ACTION:

We often build up events in our minds and then panic over what might go wrong. God does not ask us to go where he has not provided the means to help. Go where he leads, trusting him to supply courage, confidence, and resources at the right moment.

Today I will take action by:

S.W.A.G.G.

SCRIPTURE: Psalm 4:3 – "But know that the Lord has set apart for Himself him who is godly."

WORD DEFINED: **Swag -** The way in which you carry yourself. Swag is made up of your overall confidence, style, and demeanor.

IN ACTION: **S**ecure **W**hole **A**nointed **G**ifted & **G**odly

KEY WORDS:

Secure - Free from fear, anxiety, or doubt
Whole - Containing all components; complete
Anointed - dedicated to the service of God
Gifted - having great special talent or ability
Godly - conforming to the laws and wishes of God

FOOD 4 THOUGHT:

The godly are those who are faithful and devoted to God. David knew that God would hear him when he called and would answer him. We too can be confident that God listens to our prayers and answers when we call on him. Sometimes we think that God will not hear us because we have fallen short of his high standards for holy living. But if we have trusted Christ for salvation, God has forgiven us, and he will listen to us..

TAKE ACTION:

When you feel as though your prayers are bouncing off the ceiling, remember that as a believer you have been set apart by God and that he loves you. He hears and answers, although his answers may not be what you expect. Look at your problems in the light of God's power instead of looking at God in the shadow of your problems

Today I will take action by:

S.W.A.T.

SCRIPTURE: Jeremiah 29:12-13 – "Then you will call on me and come and pray to me, and I will listen to you. [13] You will seek me and find me when you seek me with all your heart."

WORD DEFINED: SWAT – Acronym used for the special weapons and tactics team.

IN ACTION: Seek **W**ait & **T**rust

KEY WORDS:

Seek - To inquire for; request
Wait - To remain or rest in expectation:
Trust - Firm reliance on the integrity, ability, or character of a person or thing

FOOD 4 THOUGHT:

God did not forget his people, even though they were captive in Babylon. He planned to give them a new beginning with a new purpose — to turn them into new people. According to God's wise plan, his people were to have hope and a future; consequently they could call upon him in confidence. Although the exiles were in a difficult place and time, they should not despair because they had God's presence, the privilege of prayer, and God's grace. Neither strange lands, sorrows, frustration, nor physical problems can break that communion.

TAKE ACTION:

In times of deep trouble, it may appear as though God has forgotten you. But God may be preparing you, as he did the people of Judah, for a new beginning with him at the center. God can be sought and found when we seek him wholeheartedly.

Today I will take action by:

V.I.S.I.O.N.

<u>SCRIPTURE:</u> Habakkuk 2:3 – "For the vision [is] yet for an appointed time, but at the end it shall speak, and not lie: though it tarry, wait for it; because it will surely come, it will not tarry."

<u>WORD DEFINED:</u> Vision - The mystical experience of seeing as if with the eyes the supernatural.

<u>IN ACTION:</u> **V**ast **I**nsight of **S**upernatural **I**nfluence **O**pposing the **N**atural

<u>KEY WORDS:</u>
<u>Vast</u> - Very great in degree or intensity
<u>Insight</u> - The capacity to discern the true nature of a situation; penetration
<u>Supernatural</u> - Of or relating to existence outside the natural world
<u>Influence</u> - A power affecting a person, thing, or course of events, especially one that operates without any direct or apparent effort
<u>Oppose</u> - To be in contention or conflict with
<u>Natural</u> - Conforming to the usual or ordinary course of nature

<u>FOOD 4 THOUGHT:</u>
God will give you a vision and a call if you ask Him to show you what He wants you to do in your life. *<u>(Taken from "Stand Strong" by Judy Jacobs)</u>*

- Waiting for your vision to be fulfilled takes patience.
- Patience conveys the idea of someone who is steadfast despite opposition or difficulty.
- If you have the vision of God, you have tapped into the source of patience for waiting.
- You are devoted to God Himself.

- God furnishes the inspiration both to wait and fulfill the vision He has given you.
- In the process of waiting He teaches you what you need to know in order to complete the picture.

James 1:4 - "Let patience have her perfect work, that you may be perfect and entire, wanting nothing."

TAKE ACTION:

Nothing needs to deter you or I. Even if we have to endure a time of seeming separations from God, when He doesn't speak to us when we are starving for His presence, the power to endure will be there-because we have a vision of God. He will sustain us when we keep our eyes on Him, waiting with patience and confidence.

Quote by Myles Munroe: "Vision is foresight with insight based on hindsight."

Today I will take action by:

____
____
____
____
____
____
____
____
____
____
____
____
____
____
____

W.A.I.T.

<u>SCRIPTURE:</u> Isaiah 64:4. – "men have not heard, nor perceived with the ear, neither has eye seen, ...what He has prepared for him that waiteth on Him."

<u>WORD DEFINED:</u> **Wait -** To stay in place in expectation of.

<u>IN ACTION:</u> **W**illfully **A**biding **I**n **T**rust

<u>KEY WORDS:</u>
<u>Willfully</u> - done deliberately
<u>Abide</u> - to endure without yielding
<u>Trust</u> - assured reliance on the character, ability, strength, or truth of someone or something

<u>FOOD 4 THOUGHT:</u>
In Habakkuk 1:2. Habakkuk had been waiting and was now at the end of his patience as this scripture reveals. Openly and honestly he approached God and asked the question: God when are you going to do something about these wicked and rebellious people of Judah. In verse 5 the Lord replied - "Look at the nations and watch-and be utterly amazed. For I am going to do something in your days that you would not believe, even if you were told." God reassured Habakkuk that He was aware of what was going on and He'd not forsaken or forgotten about him, nor was He ignoring his situation. The Lord was actually at work in the situation far beyond what Habakkuk could even imagine.

TAKE ACTION:

Are you in the WAITING room? Maybe you are awaiting an answer to a specific prayer. Maybe you are waiting for a change in circumstances, spiritual or physical healing or a revival in your church. God knows the big picture. He knows how and when He will allow everything to play out. What we want right now may not be the best thing for us right now. God has not closed His eyes to the situation; He has not forgotten us. During times when we are in the "waiting room" we have a choice: will we allow our faith to increase, or our stress? As we take our requests to God, let's approach Him in FAITH. Let's TRUST His timing and find PEACE in the knowledge that He is at work in ways far beyond what we can see.

Today I will take action by:

www.ingramcontent.com/pod-product-compliance
Ingram Content Group UK Ltd.
Pitfield, Milton Keynes, MK11 3LW, UK
UKHW020238250726
13967UKWH00001B/433